Also by Steve Kowit

*Climbing the Walls* (chapbook)
*Cutting Our Losses*
*Heart in Utter Confusion* (chapbook)
*Lurid Confessions*
*Passionate Journey*
*Pranks* (letterpress chapbook)
*Mysteries of the Body*
*For My Birthday* (chapbook)
*Epic Journeys, Unbelievable Escapes* (chapbook)

ON WRITING:

*In the Palm of Your Hand: The Poet's Portable Workshop*

ANTHOLOGIES:

*The Maverick Poets* (edited)

TRANSLATION:

*Incitement to Nixonicide and Praise for the Chilean Revolution,* by Pablo Neruda

Steve Kowit

# THE

# DUMBBELL

# NEBULA

THE ROUNDHOUSE PRESS

Publisher's Cataloging-in-Publication Data
Kowit, Steve.
The dumbbell nebula / Steve Kowit.
p. cm. — (California poetry series ; v. 3)
ISBN: 0-9666691-2-6 (PBK.)
I. Title. II. Series
PS3561.087D86 1999
811'.54 — dc21                    99-038691

Grateful acknowledgment is made to the following publications in which some of these poems, generally in earlier versions, originally appeared: *Alaska Quarterly Review, American Poets Say Goodbye to the 20th Century, Atlanta Review, Caprice, Exquisite Corpse, Hiram Poetry Review, Mangrove, The Mickle Street Review, The New Yorker, The New York Quarterly, Onthebus, Ploughshares, Poetry Flash, Poets for Life, River Styx, Scarp, The Sierra Madre Review,* and *The Spirit That Moves Us.* In addition, some of these poems were first printed in small collections published by Bloody Twin Press, Uroboros Books, Caernarvon Press, and State Street Press, and in a larger collection published by Carpenter Press.

This is Volume 3 of the California Poetry Series.
Cover Photo: Brad Ehrhorn
Author Photo: Tina Wegener
Cover and Interior Design: David Bullen Design

The California Poetry Series is published by The Roundhouse Press
and distributed by Heyday Books.

Orders, inquiries, and correspondence should be addressed to:
Heyday Books
P.O. Box 9145
Berkeley, California 94709
phone: 510.549.3564  fax: 510.549.1889
e-mail: roundhouse@heydaybooks.com

Printed in Canada
10  9  8  7  6  5  4  3  2  1

# Contents

*For Mary & in memory of my parents*

In the hall of pain,
what abundance on the table.

CZESLAW MILOSZ

## A Trick

Late afternoon. Huancayo. We'd made the long haul down
from Ayacucho that morning. Were hungry & tired.
Had stumbled into one of those huge, operatic, down-at-the-heels
Peruvian restaurants: red cloths on the tables, teardrop
chandeliers, candles in ribbed silver cages.
Its back wall the remains of an ancient Quechua temple:
that massive, mortarless, perfectly fitted hand-hewn stone
whose secret had died with the Incas.
The place was deserted, except for a middle-aged waiter
tricked out in the shabby black & white jacket
& slacks of the trade. He brought us two menus,
two goblets for wine, a plate of *papas a la huancaina.*
I was unaccountably happy. In one of those giddy,
insouciant moods that come out of nowhere.
The previous summer I'd given the army the slip,
leaving to better men than myself the task of carpet-bombing
the indigent peasants of Asia.
Mary & I had exchanged matrimonial vows in Seattle
& then headed south. Had been bussing for months
from town to town thru the Andes.
The truth is, the whole thing had happened by magic.
                                        "Hey,
you know that trick where you blow an invisible coin
into a sealed-up glass?" I lowered a saucer over her long-
stemmed goblet so nothing could enter, & grinned
as if I knew how to pluck out of nowhere fishes & loaves.
Mary said No, she didn't—& laughed,
preparing herself for another fine piece of buffoonery.
On the table between us, though it wasn't yet dark,
the candle was already lit. In the distance, the misty sierra.

I asked her to hand me a coin, placed it into my palm,
recited some hocus-pocus known only to shamans from Brooklyn,
then spread out my fingers—& lo & behold, it had vanished!
So far so good. But that part was easy. What I did next
was harder—to blow the invisible coin into that covered-up glass.
The nice thing was you could see it fall in with a clatter,
hear the luxurious clink of silver in glass as it dropped
out of nowhere & settled. Needless to say, she was amazed.
I mean *really* amazed! & so too was our waiter
who, as it turns out, had been watching the whole affair
from the wall by the kitchen, & flew to my side
flailing his arms like a sinner whose soul the Holy
Spirit had entered, & who knows he is saved.
He wanted to know how I'd done it. How such a thing
could possibly happen. *Milagro!* I felt like Jesus
raising the dead: a little embarrassed, but pleased
that I'd brought the thing off—& that someone had seen it.
Huancayo. I liked the looks of the place: that sharp
mountain light before dusk, folks walking around
on the other side of the window in woolen serapes.
If it wouldn't have sounded so pious
or grandiose, I'd have said to that fellow: "Friend,
how I did it isn't really the point; in this world nothing
is more or less marvelous than anything else."
But I didn't. Instead, I just shrugged, the way
that when Lazarus opened his eyes & shook off the dust
& put on his hat, Jesus himself must have shrugged,
as much as to say it was nothing, a trifle. & that done,
we checked out the menus, & taking our new friend's advice
ordered a huge vegetarian feast—me & Mary, my wife,
that woman who one day—all wit & forbearance
& grace—had fallen, by some sort of miracle, into my life.

# I Rendezvous with Jim & Lenny at the Barnes

We swept up everything in sight: gobbled up Soutines, Bonnards,
Modiglianis. Lenny snagged Monet's boat studio.
Jim seized that mauve felicity of creamy lovers: *Le bonheur
de vivre.* I took that terrifying Van Gogh nude,
horrific & farouche—all poverty & pubic hair & suffering.
Together after all those years—three
hebephrenic & disheveled antiquarian collectors
from the Dumbbell Nebula.
The museum-goers gave us a wide berth.
The guards eyed us suspiciously & shifted feet.
At closing time we slipped into our coats & left
our acquisitions where they'd hung,
& traipsed out into an icy dusk.
In Philadelphia, on Earth, all afternoon,
it had been snowing: a foamy, plush, untouched
meringue of snow, all lacy-blue beneath the streetlights,
blanketing the lawns & trees & roofs
& roads of Lower Merion, flakes huge as pie crusts
floating all about us as we clowned
& schmoozed the way we used to
carry on back in Manhattan down on 6th Street
in the old days, nothing now but tiny strokes
of silver-gray & orange & maroon, receding
past the middle distance—rapturous,
maniacal—high-stepping thru a blizzard of exquisite light.

## Meet the Poet Laureate

Because of my uncanny physical resemblance to Richard Wilbur
people often stop me on the street to shake my hand
& say how pleased they are to meet the Poet Laureate
of the United States.
                            "No, no!" I say at once,
"Why, I'm the one who should feel privileged!"
The upshot is they think I would do well
to turn the story of their life into a poem:
                            "Dick, just before the end, so frail & thin
that she can hardly walk, she whispers, 'Mike,
let's take a boat out like we used to.'
At first I hesitate, but then I think: Okay, why not.
So there we are, drifting down the Colorado like the old days,
& it's marvelous. She leaning on my shoulder with that sleepy grin.
At sunset all those colors & then everything grows hazy
—you know how it does—& dark,
& when I start to weep she lifts my hand up to her lips & whispers:
'Mike, I'm happy. Don't be sad.' & just
then, at the very moment that I take her in my arms
for that last time,
                            an enormous orange moon
drifts up above the aspens, out of nowhere . . ."

I shake my head. There's nothing I can say.
They corner me in laundromats & bookstores, lobbies of hotels.
There was the guy who watched his wife pick up a gun
& blow her brains out,
& the lady from Laguna Beach whose husband had been shoved
out of a truck by Mafia goons. The fellow
who had watched his wife die in a relocation camp for Japanese.
A woman who had shaved her head & tried to kill herself
& spent two decades in a hospital for the insane.

They stop me on the street, in parks, at airports,
under the marquees of movie theaters in the rain.
The paraplegic who had been a pilot.
The dancer who had cured herself of multiple sclerosis.
Brothers reunited after thirty years.
The one who'd lost the left side of her face
for having pulled a stranger from a flaming car. "No one
who had heard those screams," she said to me,
"could have done less."
—Miracles. Astounding transformations.
Tales of epic journeys, unbelievable escapes.
Prodigious talent crushed by circumstance or whiskey or cocaine.
They stop me on the street. They want to talk. They want
to buy me coffee, dinner, drinks. "It must be a terrific thing
to be the Poet Laureate," they say.
"I could have been a writer too. But listen, Dick,
here's something that you won't believe—" & then,
before I can protest, they're into it. The woman
who had managed to slip out of Poland
when she was twelve & never saw her family again.
The ex-con from the Mosquito Coast who fell in love with Mayan glyphs.
The shoe store clerk who had been Waltz King of America.
The chap who told his wife that he was homosexual
& lay down on a country road & wept.
As soon as they start in I'm done for, hooked.
I want to weep, embrace them, tell them that I understand completely.
Let them know how terrible I feel.
Or that I'm overjoyed it all worked out.
They walk right up and introduce themselves & shake my hand.
They stammer & gesticulate, insisting it would make the most terrific poem.
& I say yes, it would. By God,
I have a mind to start on it at once—this very evening.
& that, of course, pleases them immensely.
It's the least I can do.
We hug goodbye. "Dick, take care . . . & don't forget
to get that orange moon into the poem—that moon
above the aspens. Hell,

it just says everything, you know?"
& I say yes, of course. For heaven's sake,
don't worry about that. That isn't something that I'm likely to forget.
No way I'd leave the moon out of that poem.

# Kiss

On the patio of that little cafe in the Del Mar Plaza
across from the Esmeralda Bookstore, where you can
sit sipping latté & look out past the Pacific
Coast Highway onto the ocean, a couple is tangled
in one of those steamy, smoldering kisses.
His right arm coils her waist, arching her back
& drawing her toward him. He could be Sicilian,
or Lebanese, with that gorgeous complexion,
those chiseled forearms, that clutch of dark curls.
The young woman's skirt, lilac & sheer, lifts
as she stretches, levitated out of her sandals, out
of her body, her head flung back, fingers
wrapped in his curls. Her long chestnut hair
spills toward her thighs as she clings to his mouth,
to his loins, to his chest. How wickedly
beautiful both of them are! To their left,
off the North County coast, on an infinite sea,
two sailboats triangulate heaven. In the sheen
of the morning, you munch an apricot scone
& sip your cafe latté, that blue cup of light at your lips,
with its genie of steam. In its vase, on your table,
a white tea rose shimmers. Your fork
shines on its plate. Everything trembles & glows.

## Metaphysics

The trouble with me is I have a low metaphysical threshold.
When I'm told the bicameral mind can never know things in themselves,
I shake my head gravely . . . but simply out of politeness.
Frankly, the conflict between the noumenal & phenomenal worlds
means nothing to me whatsoever.
*Is perceptual knowledge constrained by the categorical space*
*in which language unfolds,*
*or is Absolute Is-ness provoked by the Relative Ought?*
"Well, I'd never quite thought of things in that light . . ."
I stammer & cough. I help myself to the cheese dip.
Perhaps I'm obtuse, but I could never recall whether it's Essence
that precedes Existence, or the other way round.
The fact is I'd rather my pinky get slammed in the door of a semi
than argue over the epistemological underpinnings of post-deconstruction,
whether signifiers are self-referential, or meaning culture-specific.
It's knotty alright, I say, stifling a yawn.
The question of course is who is that redhead,
the one at the other end of the room with the lavender
lipstick & radical décolletage?
& why at these awful soirees do I always get stuck among the professors?
If it isn't free-will, they are beating to death the mind-body dilemma,
the transcendental nature of Time, that gut-wrenching issue:
does or does not the external world really exist?
Ah, now she is crossing her legs!
I help myself to the pretzels. I pour some more wine.
Let them build the City of God out of earwax & toothpicks without me.
*And what, pray tell, is the meaning of Meaning?*
*Are Existence & Nothingness one & the same?*
*And how in the Bright Night of Dread does the body of Ontic Being arise?*
I shake my head, as much as to say I too am perplexed.
Politeness itself, I am loath to point out that perhaps what we need
is more daylight & less metaphysics.
As if this world isn't perfectly real as it is, or as real as it gets,
they want us to think that the world behind it is better,

that the dead are elsewhere & happy,
that our loved ones are waiting for us on the other side of *samsara*.
As if that sort of cerebral monoxide could stifle
the groans of the dying, the winds of disaster, the weeping
that's left here behind us. & still they go on.
Armageddon itself would not be enough to dissuade them!
*Is Spirit immortal? Do dreams occupy space?*
*Is the universe purposeful, random, unbounded, autogenous, finite, alive?*
*Is death an illusion? Or simply another sort of beginning?*
*A journey indeed—but whither & whence?*
Yes, yes! I say, my head spinning.
It's utterly fascinating! Who would have guessed it!
Far off in the night, a coyote howls at the moon.
I have by now finished the cheese dip, the pretzels, the wine.
The lickerish redhead has long since slipped off
on the arms of her lover—some young, good-looking swine.
I rise with a hundred regrets, thanking my hosts,
zipping my jacket, & spouting farewells in every direction:
It's certainly something to ponder, I tell them,
but really, I have to get going.
It's late & tomorrow I'm up bright & early.
A marvelous evening! Your quiche by the way was divine!

## View of Toledo

I guess I don't like this planet a whole lot, my wife said
in that quiet way that she has—
that tone of irreconcilable sadness that's so
much a part of her nature.
It was the death of our neighbor, the old guy upstairs
in 4C, that had started her in.
It always scares me a bit when she says
things like that.
                "C'mon," I suggested,
"let's stroll down by the beach & pick up a paper."
But outside, the world wasn't any more rosy:
palm trees dying of some kind of blight were waving
goodbye, while street lamps stood near them, heads
bowed like shy anorexics.
The surf, pounding away like that in the dark,
wasn't the least bit consoling.
"Do you think that's Venus up there?" she asked,
  looking up at the one bright patch in the night.
"Yep," I said, "it sure is. You know,
  Venus is over one hundred & fifty miles away!
  Which is why it looks so small from down here.
  Actually, it's about the size of Toledo, Ohio."
We stood there a moment, gazing
up at the sky—those vast black stretches
with only a handful of lights in between.
"The odd thing is, the folks who live
  there do everything backwards," I went on.
"Really? Like what?"
"Well, for one thing, they wear socks on their heads,
  & they eat with their toes,
  & the older they grow the younger they get
  till they're nothing but kids skating around in the parks."
She was, of course, tickled to hear it:
a place that much different from this one.

She took my hand & we walked to the seawall
in absolute silence. Then we stopped
& she kissed me, right there in the dark
by that dumb beach where the sand
is so crummy it falls apart in your hands,
& the harebrained Atlantic is all thumbs,
banging forever into the Florida coast.

## Cutting Our Losses

In a downtown San José hotel,
exhausted & uptight & almost broke,
we blew 16 *colones* & got stewed on rum.
You lounged in bed
reading *Hermelinda Linda* comics
while I stumbled drunk around the room
complaining
& reciting poems out of an old anthology.
I read that Easter elegy of Yeats,
which moved you,
bringing back that friend of yours,
Bob Fishman, who was dead.
You wept. I felt terrible.
We killed the bottle, made a blithered
kind of love & fell asleep.
Out in the Costa Rican night
the weasels of the dark held a fiesta
celebrating our safe arrival in their city
& our sound sleep.
We found our Ford Econoline
next morning where we'd left it,
on a side street, but ripped
apart like a piñata,
like a tortured bird, wing
window busted in, a door
sprung open on its pins like an astonished beak.
Beloved, everything we lost: our old blues
tapes, the telephoto lens, the Mayan priest,
that ancient Royal portable I loved,
awoke me to how tentative & delicate
& brief & precious it all is, & was
for that a sort of aphrodisiac—though bitter
to swallow. That evening,
drunk on loss, I loved you

wildly, with a crazy passion, knowing
as I did, at last, the secret
of your own quietly voluptuous heart—you
who have loved always with a desperation
born as much of sorrow as of lust,
being, I suppose, at once unluckier,
& that much wiser to begin with.

# Rain

When we were good & done
again she slid the towel
down to dry herself, then
sat up lazily
to pour another glass
of Beaujolais
from the decanter
by the stereo.
From where I lay
I watched the notched
spine of her back,
her hair, which earlier,
as she had taken
out the pins, had fallen
in such lovely disarray
against her shoulders.
When she curled back
down we lay there
for a long while
listening
to the slush of tires
on the street—
the rain that beat
against the rocks
out in the courtyard
& was dripping
down the eaves.
"It's perfect, isn't it?"
she whispered,
snuggling up
against me. "Just
what we've been

needing all this time—
a good
hard
all-day rain."

## For My Birthday

Friends, a moment ago, standing here at the table, ready to blow out the candles,
it came to me—if it's true what you say, & I do indeed seem to grow younger
with each passing year, then in no time at all Mary & I will be back
in that Ocean Beach duplex, with its rapture of white camellias,
my vertigo gone & my lower spine supple again,
& my hearing & sight as sharp as ever they'd been,
& Sally & JayJay will still be alive, & Binky & Ivan purring away on the sofa.
Outside, the Pacific pounding the cliffs with its ancient, millennial music,
an exaltation of sea-nymphs, & surfers
bobbing like half-notes out past the breakers;
the heart a blue frisbee spinning over that beach from Pescadero to Brighton.
If you're right & I keep growing younger I'll find myself back in the Andes:
Esmeraldas. The rains of Tumaco. The Popayán hills in the misty weeping of dawn.
That thundering gorge into Baños. The road thru the steaming Petén to Tikal.
                              —It is morning. Chiapas. Your voice as it was, rising
over that rosewood guitar that you loved so, in that courtyard of wild datura.
McHenry. The Sandias at sunset. The two of us young again
in that railroad flat in the Fillmore, our bodies entwined in the dark.
Cold peaches in moonlight. The Avalon Ballroom. —To be with them
again, those who disappeared across borders & oceans, into anonymous cities,
ashrams, communes—Phoenix House, prison, the Cuetzalan mist.
Seen for the last time on a street in downtown Seattle, Lima, Panajachel—
Jeremy . . . Franklin . . . Gregory . . . Owen . . . Elizabeth back in Manhattan Beach—
all that impossible beauty.
                                        Death, with its hacking cough
& its cryptic shudder, its final ambiguous phone call.
Death suddenly sitting up in its bed. Death with a spike in the vein, the husk
of the spirit slumped at the wheel of a Buick somewhere in Tucson.
Half a century's streamer of blood in the rain.
The unending immolation of Asia. The cakewalk of black mortification.
Cows swinging from hooks; rabbits blinded for one more cream blusher
& lipstick; dogs in terminal agony circling their cages. Isaac
Bashevis Singer was right: for the animals every day is Treblinka.
To be back on the streets again agitating & marching—What else is there for it?

Dearest, if every year I grow younger,
does that mean that someday I'll find myself back in Manhattan without you?
Your name strange to my lips. Not even to know you exist.
That you stand at the cusp of the future, waiting for me in its shadows. Beloved,
I do not think that I wish to be back there without you.
It's simply out of the question—I absolutely refuse—I . . . Agh! what am I saying—
Nothing will stop it. I'll float thru the Village with Murray at midnight,
past the old Cedar Bar, Les Deux Megots, the rippled winos of Third Avenue
curled in their doorways. Past the painted Ukrainian eggs of the Lower East Side.
Past Tompkins Square Park. That I climb the six flights of that walk-up
on Avenue B. All that music & *mishegas* & metaphysical fervor.
Night lit with its incense & tongues, its muted horn & its velvet drum.
Night with its muffled cries in the dark.
O soft-limbed lost girls of my youth, how purely this time around I will love you.
                    Let it snow again on the Hudson!
Let the sirens wail & the busses belch & the tugs
on the East River sound their guttural honks. Let the poetry readings begin once again
at Le Metro—Ed Sanders & Mickey Ruskin presiding. Let the streets of Manhattan
hum again with its poets & waifs & musicians & mad action painters,
its feverish vanguard of doomed & beautiful women.
Let the Puerto Rican domino players squat on their crates outside their *bodegas*
under the bulging piñata of sunlight, let their voluptuous daughters
promenade thru the streets & their sons sing five-part harmony
in the echo-chambered tenement hallways of 6th Street.
This time around I'll listen more raptly. This time I'll know what I'm hearing.
This time I won't miss a beat.
                    8th Street at Fifth. McDougal & Bleeker.
Mott & Canal. To cross Crane's bridge out of Brooklyn again—cathedral & harp
over the river into downtown ruckus Manhattan. White buildings
lit with the golden palette of morning. The guts of a disemboweled piano
strummed on a vacant street in the roseate dawn of the 60s—*Missa Benedicta*
of Avenue C—crescendo of taxis & busses.
Let Cassidy knock again at my door. Let him harangue me once more
with his breathless paean to Mao. Let Rozzie awaken beside me.
Let Lenny regale me with one of his endless apocryphal tales of Bonnard & Monet
as we hoof it back from Penn Station—
Yes, yes, I say. Very true! Absolutely the case!

We are lost in the bright air of impossible gaiety, incomparable youth,
jubilatio of camaraderie, passion & blather, that feast made of fine talk.
Let me wrangle with Jim over Wittgenstein's last proposition. That's what I want,
to yammer all night over that which cannot be said! Wax ecstatic
with Jack on one of those long evening strolls around Sheepshead Bay—
Drunken boats of our Brooklyn boyhoods—the two of us cooked to the gills
on Céline & Rimbaud & Miller & Crane & Genet.

                                                 That house on 14th Street.
It's just a matter of time till I'm back there again.
My folks in the doorway—vital & young.
All morning I stand by that maple tree out by the curb, its bronze plaque
announcing that somebody's son had been killed in the War:
just a name & some dates, like this poem, reminder that somebody lived.
To stand dumbstruck with love of a schoolgirl whose name has been swallowed
up by the decades. No matter. Let me return to worship her image again.
Let my mother yak on the phone with my grandmother, Bertha,
impoverished lame widowed immigrant girl of the *shtetls* of Poland.
Listen. You can hear it. The two of them gabbing away together in Yiddish.
Dad in the backyard, laconic & patient, up on that rickety paint-splattered ladder.
He's putting the screens up for summer. The garden a bliss of roses & mums.
How good they both look! How delighted & young! Just a couple of kids!
I swear it, they've never looked better! happier! younger!
I tell you I can't wait to be back there, though it's half a century yet down the pike!
A curly-haired kid staring out thru the window at sunset over the backyards
of Flatbush, full of unnameable longing, in love with the burnished light
of late afternoon. The Brighton Express in the distance. That cradle of wires.
The pigeons & sparrows. The rolling past of the clouds. Unspeakable
intimations of what they might mean.
—Birthdays yes, but no such thing as goodbyes!
In love, though I didn't know it then, with the whole inexplicable business.
First sorrow & first wisdom. A mote of molecular dust, like an ant on a leaf,
blown across infinite seas.  —To be here at all! To have bubbled up out of the void!
Who would have guessed it?

                          Friends, thank you for coming.
Doesn't the cake look delicious?
For myself, of course, I am absolutely delighted to be here among you.
Immeasurably pleased. Thickening paunch, stiffening joints, vertigo, bum back,

wrecked hearing & sight notwithstanding.

Alive nonetheless! —All of us! —Here in this strange, unspeakably marvelous life.

& Mary, companion & love, here beside me.

A wish? Friends, what on earth more could I wish for?

Like you say—every year I grow younger. So be it!

Okay, are you ready? Hush now. . . . I'm going to blow out the candles.

## Josephine's Garden

First thing in the morning the phone rings.
& Mary tells me that Jack,
who's been dying of AIDS for two years,
is finally gone.
An hour later the ophthalmologist
puts some sort of drops in my eyes
& for the rest of the day
the light is blinding.
When I go outside I have to wear
those dark paper shades the nurse gave me.
Even the pulpy gray stones
& the faded hedge & the pale green spikes
of the barrel cactus
in Josephine's garden
are too bright to look at,
while her roses & bougainvillea
blaze out as if someone
had suddenly flung back the shutters—as
blinding as one of those high-
mountain blizzards,
but more gorgeous & painful.
If this is the way the world really is
it's too much to look at.
No one could ever survive it.
Nevertheless, all afternoon,
I keep stepping out into that garden,
eyes smarting as if someone
had rinsed them in acid,
astonished again
at the unbelievable colors,
the utter profusion of forms,
the sharp edges everything has in this world.

## II  MYSTERIES

### Beetles

> The famous British biologist J.B.S. Haldane, when asked by
> a churchman ... to state his conception of God, said: "He is
> inordinately fond of beetles."
>> *Primo Levi*

Spotted blister beetles. Sacred scarabs.
Water beetles whirling on the surface of still ponds.
Little polkadotted ladybugs
favored by the Virgin Mary & beloved of children.
Those angelic fireflies sparkling in the summer evenings.
Carrion beetles sniffing out the dead.
June bugs banging into screens.
Click beetles. Tumblebugs. Opossum beetles. Whirligigs
& long-horned rhino beetles.
Cowpea weevils snuggling into beans.
The diving beetle wintering in mud.
*Macrodactylus subspinosus*: the rose chafer
feasting upon rose petals, dear to the poet Guido Gozzano.
The reddish-brown *Calathus gregarius*.
Iridescent golden brown-haired beetles.
Beetles living in sea wrack, dry wood, loose gravel.
Clown beetles. Pill beetles.
Infinitesimal beetles nesting in the spore tubes of fungi.
There is no climate in which the beetle does not exist,
no ecological niche the beetle does not inhabit,
no organic matter, living, dead, or decomposed
that has not its enthusiast among the beetles,
of whom, it has been estimated, one and one-half
million species currently exist,
which is to say one mortal creature
out of five's a beetle—little armored tank

who has been rolling through the fields her ball of dung
these past three hundred million years: clumsy
but industrious, powerful yet meek,
the lowly, dutiful, & unassuming beetle—
she of whom, among all earth-born creatures, God is fondest.

## Perognathus fallax

When I went to the shed to check for water damage
after the last rains,
I found a tiny gray mouse, dead
among the rubbish of an old carton,
& lifting out the rags & jars, came
on his mate, backed in a corner, tiny
and alive. Beside her—ears
barely visible flecks, tails nothing
but tendrils of gray thread—two nurslings:
one curled asleep by her snout,
& the other awake at her nipple;
the three together no larger, I'd guess,
than the height of my thumb.
I took the box into the yard,
where there was more light,
& where the cats weren't lurking,
& lifted out the rest of the detritus—
a shredded pillow, cans of varnish
& spray paint—beneath which I found, woven
out of what must have been pieces
of cotton, chewed cardboard, & small twigs,
some sort of ramshackle nest.
Now, with nowhere to hide,
she scurried behind it, a pup still at her dugs,
& looked up at me, into my eyes,
the way one of my cats might
who'd been cornered, or as might
one of my own kind, pleading—
her gaze wholly human, wholly intelligible.
It's uncanny, isn't it,
how much alike we all are?
The next morning,
when I went to the pump house
where I'd set the carton for safety,

I was amazed to see the perfect
filigreed globe into which
she had rewoven her nest overnight—
From a port at its top, her tiny snout,
& those two bright eyes
peering anxiously up into my face.
I just stood there: I could hardly believe
how exquisite that nest was,
& how happy I was to see her.
The crumbs of seed I had dropped in
were gone, & I couldn't help but think
how nice it would be
to keep them there, safe from the hawks,
feed them whatever they liked—
but for only a moment.
Then took out my knife
& sliced a small hole in the cardboard,
an inch or so from the bottom,
& the next time I went back they were gone.
I was sorry to see the thing empty.
Is that stupid of me? *Perognathus*
*fallax*: the San Diego pocket mouse,
according to my *Audubon*
*Guide to North American Mammals*—
which was the last week of March,
the whole yard given over to mountain lilac
& sage & alyssum
& out by the wood fence, that stand of iris,
too tattered, I'd thought, to survive
all those hard rains,
but which had.
& under my feet, alive, but so tiny
one hardly noticed,
a hundred species of wild flower:
saffron & white & pink & mauve & blood red.

## Field Notes

A pandemonium of local birders
(*Ornithologicus californicus*)
swoops down
on Peñasquitos Lagoon,
terrifying every other creature
into flight.
Appears—despite
ungainly girth,
interminable gabble,
goggly eyes, & waddling gait—
comparatively harmless.
A kind of domestic loon.

## Ronnie

Shortly after they'd scrambled his brain with electroshock,
I bumped into him on a Brooklyn street.
He had put on some weight, seemed calmer, less jangled.
No longer the manic young poet who'd bounce
about on the balls of his feet, barely touching
the street as he floated above it,
he had tricked back that garland of black curls,
sported, of all things, a jacket & tie,
& seemed, for once, at home in his body—grounded
the way the rest of us are, by the world's weight.
      "Steve, I feel great!"
though his voice, too quick & emphatic,
made me uneasy: "A million times better off—"
And he opened his fist in a little explosion of fingers & thumb,
by way of dismissing, as if it hadn't really been his,
that earlier life:
    "Though sometimes . . . I . . .
I guess I forget things. . . ." & with that
it collapsed: the sanguine, implacable mask electro-
convulsive shock had made of his face
crumbled along the line of his mouth, & his eyes went hazy.
He looked scared, like a man who wakes up
& doesn't know where he is, his own name, what city
he's in, or whose body: that old,
impetuous storm squelched to a kind of stolid confusion.
    *The northeast heaves,*
   *O loveliest of winds to me—*
a line from one of his exquisite Hölderlin versions
swam through my head. The street glistened with rain.
Leaves spun at our feet. Yes, I said, it was true, I was
leaving New York. We made the sort of talk
people make. Shook hands: "Ronnie,
it's great to see you again!" Only an awkward civility
kept me from hugging him, weeping—& then hurried off,

though thirty years later, having just heard he was gone,
I set the phone to its cradle & stand
in the dark, wrenched back to that street
& to all that had never got said—the sorrow
& love I had left there, unspoken between us:
his fitful, disquieted spirit; the poem of his life
whirling about in my  head—a tumult of leaves
in a gust of uneasy wind.

## Crossing the Desert

Finally I got up & walked over to the couple at the next
fire ring. "Look," I said quietly, "I'm trying to sleep."
"Pal," the guy looked up, "this here is our
campsite & we'll talk as long as we goddam feel like."
He had on a blue Padres cap & was sprawled out
in the tent on his belly, with a six-pack of Coors,
& she was outside on a folding chair by the fishing rods,
swinging a leg that was marble in the moonlight.
The last thing I needed was trouble, but I took a step
toward him anyhow. "It's midnight," I said, hunkering down.
"I don't think you have any idea how—"
"Buddy," he raised himself on one elbow, "I'll tell you this
one last fucking time—" But I turned around & walked off.
In the dark, among strangers, you never know
what can happen. He must have thought I was going back
for a pipe-wrench, or my .22, because there wasn't
a sound after that. I dragged my mummy bag
out of the tent & as I lay there in the stillness,
circled by the silhouettes of camper shells
& Winnebagos, everything grew suddenly strange—as if,
unmoored from time, I'd stumbled on the ruins
of some ancient caravan. A savage & nomadic people
is how they'll remember us a thousand years from now
when we're not even dust anymore, is what I was thinking,
lying there under those billion stars, the silence broken
only by the thin, electric buzz of the cicadas, wind
rasping in the chaparral, & what must have been
the canopy of someone's tent out in the darkness, flapping.

## Refugees, Late Summer Night

Woke with a start, the dogs barking out by the fence,
yard flooded with light. Groped to the window.
Out on the road a dozen quick figures
hugging the shadows: bundles slung at their shoulders,
water jugs at their hips. You could hear,
under the rattle of wind, as they passed,
the crunch of sneakers on gravel. *Pollos.* Illegals
who'd managed to slip past the border patrol,
its Broncos & choppers endlessly circling
the canyons & hills between here & Tecate.
Out there, in the dark, they could have been
anyone: refugees from Rwanda, slaves pushing north.
Palestinians, Gypsies, Armenians, Jews. . . .
The lights of Tijuana, that yellow haze to the west,
could have been Melos, Cracow, Quang Ngai. . . .
I watched from the window till they were lost
in the shadows. Our motion light turned itself off.
The dogs gave a last, perfunctory bark
& loped back to the house; those dry, rocky hills
& the wild sage at the edge of the canyon
vanishing too. Then stared out at nothing.
No sound anymore but my own breath,
& the papery click of the wind in the leaves
of that parched eucalyptus: a rattle of bones;
chimes in a doorway; history riffling its pages.

## Romero

By early December the dirt road will be nicely macadamed,
& the backcountry dust will no longer blow through the window
into my hair. In the chill of the oncoming winter
I'll rise from my chair & throw pitch pine & oak on the fire—look,
it is nearly winter already! By now Romero
should either be up around Fresno, working construction,
or back in Tuxtla Gutiérrez, yoked to a cart of *paletas*
& mending his socks—& plotting another go at the States.
When he stepped from the canyon I pulled to the shoulder
& opened the door. We were north of Tecate: the border patrol
swarming over the highway. Did I have any neighbor,
he wanted to know, who needed a worker?
So all morning, at my place, we cut back the wild chamise
by the shed, though we ended up arguing over money:
he wouldn't take a cent. That was to pay me for picking him up
in the first place. "Romero, for god's sakes
you can't work for nothing!"—& kept at him until he relented.
Mary, what fine enchiladas! what heavenly pears!
How exhausted he was, & dusty & hungry & hopeful!
Late in the evening we wove our way out of the mountains:
the Barrett grade thru Dulzura down to Spring Valley
& north to Santee. It was August. The night sky a bucket
of coins spilling over the hills. Now & then meteors
flared thru the darkness & vanished. "Right here
is good," he said on a back street, at a grove of black
eucalyptus. I pulled to the curb. It was where he would sleep.
In the morning, a truck cruising Magnolia
would take him to Fresno,
where *la migra* was scarce & plenty of guys like himself,
without papers, were working construction. He slung his blanket
over his shoulder, picked up his bag, & asked me again
in his broken, measured, tentative English, please
to thank my *Maria bonita* for all of her kindness. I said that I would.
"Romero, take care. . . ." & under those fugitive stars

we gave each other a long, final *abrazo*. Country
of endless abundance & workers with nowhere to sleep.
"Esteban, I. . . ." —& he nodded, & turned,
& walked off into that tunnel of trees & was gone.

## Basic

The first thing that they do is shave your head
& scream into your face until you drop
the pleasant fiction that had been your life.
More quickly than you would have guessed
you learn obedience: to shut your mouth
& do what you are told; that you survive
by virtue of compliance, shutting down.
When they scream "drop for twenty" then you drop.
If wobbly from lack of sleep,
you're told to sit up half the night & strip
your M-1 down, that's what you do: you strip it down.
The only insubordination's in your eyes, that can't
accept the order not to close. Your combat boots
kept so compulsively spit-shined
you see your face in both hard toes—skinned
to the scalp, pathetically distorted,
not unrecognizable but not quite you—a self
that marches dutifully through sleet & has perfected
the low crawl.
                    One gray morning in the second week
of basic training, lacing up his boots,
that shy, phlegmatic red-haired boy who bunked
above me whispered
                                        "Steve,
I don't believe I'm gonna make it. . . ."
"No way man! You're doing fine! . . . Hey look, c'mon, we're late,"
& shrugged him off to race out just in time
to make formation in the mist
of that Kentucky morning.
—He was right. He didn't. He took a razor blade that night,
& crawling underneath the barracks slashed his throat.
What little of myself I saved in there
I saved by tiny gestures of defiance:
Instead of screaming *Kill*, I'd plunge my bayonet

into that dummy, screaming *Quill . . . Nil. . . .*
At rifle drill I'd hum the *Internationale*
& fire fifty feet above the target. I kept Dexedrines
in my fatigues. Took heart from the seditious drollery
of Sergeant May, that L.A. homeboy
with the black goatee, all hip panache & grace:
that bop salute & smart-ass version of left-face.
& sometimes from his cadre room at night, the wailing
blues of Ray Charles drifted through the barracks
& I'd lie there in the dark, awake—remembering
that other life that I had left behind.
& it was Sergeant May & Ray Charles
& Dexedrine that got me through.
Had I been more courageous, less the terrified recruit
who did what he was told, I would have hung back
with that boy & argued with him,
said whatever needed saying
or at least have heard him out, just listened, or let someone
know, or somehow, god knows, saved him.
But I wasn't. & I didn't.
I was just a kid myself.
For all my revolutionary rhetoric, I shut my eyes
& ears, when shutting of the eyes & ears was politic.
When they said strip your M-1 down, I stripped it down.
When they said march, I marched.

# The Black Shoe

A couple of newlyweds, up at the Del Mar station,
saw the woman stumble & fall, & ran back
to pull her to safety, the train bearing down.
For a thousand feet north of the point of impact,
investigators found parts of a briefcase, sketches
of gowns, a low-heeled black shoe. From
the White House, the President screaming for blood.
A quarter million American boys already shipped
to the Gulf. No doubt some of the kids
from the base: Mike Santos & Tracy & Kevin, horsing
around like they used to in class—a football
spiraling over the Saudi Arabian sands. At night,
unable to sleep, tossing in bed, I hatch extravagant plots
to bring the ship of state down. I am determined
that not a single one of my students shall die;
not a single Iraqi infant be orphaned
or murdered. Such are the feverish thoughts
that spin thru my head in that fugue state
before sleep lifts me out of myself & carries me off.
In the morning, however, it isn't the President
circled by microphones, screeching for war,
that throbs in my head, but that unstoppable train,
& the fact that both women were killed: the one
who'd just gotten married reaching her arms
to the arms of the one who had stumbled
& fallen. It won't let me rest. The briefcase.
Those bloody sketches of gowns. That black shoe.

## Alpha Centauri

We were down at the Hungry Hunter's
after a peace march, when Danny,
whose passions are social justice
& roast Cornish hen,
starts whipping himself into a frenzy
over the President's lies,
multinational greed,
the Pentagon's homicidal agenda.
"The exploitation of anyone,"
Danny says, lifting that small bird's body
in both of his hands
& tearing a wing off,
"oppresses us all!"
& with that he starts in on the rape of the Congo,
slavery in Cape Town,
torture in Turkey,
El Salvador,
Poland,
Afghanistan,
Alpha Centauri . . .
Ripping the last bit of flesh with his teeth,
Danny says there are millions
of corpses
under our noses
that nobody sees.
& when everyone else at the table agrees,
he shakes his head as much as to say
it's beyond comprehension,
& wipes a trickle of grease from his chin,
& crumples his napkin onto a plate
full of bones & pieces of skin
& leftover peas.

## Friendly Persuasion

When I mentioned to Carl that I was convinced
we Homo sapiens have a biological impulse to murder—
that the hunt & the kill are not simply culture-conditioned
but coded into the DNA,
that our lust for slaughter is clearly a zoological
fact that any objective observer
would note from the start,
he leapt to his feet & flew at me screaming:

                                           "Kowit

you've been brainwashed by Jansen & Shockley
& all the other sociobiological hirelings
of the corporate state—
that phalangist cabal of pseudo-scientific apologists
for the criminal right!"
He lifted his fist in the air & shook it, raging
& baring his teeth,
his face suddenly bestial & savage.
I drew back, daring to say not a single word more
in defense of what was, after all, only a theory.
I mean the motherfucker was ready to kill me!

# Mysteries

Tonight, sick with the flu & alone, I drift in confusion & neurasthenia
surrendering to the chaos & mystery of all things,
for tonight it comes to me like a sad but obvious revelation
that we know nothing at all.
Despite all our fine theories we don't have the foggiest notion
of why or how anything in this world exists
or what anything means or how anything fits
or what we or anyone else are doing here in the first place.
Tonight the whole business is simply beyond me.
Painfully I sit up in bed & look out the window into the evening.
There is a light on in Marie's apartment.
My neighbor Marie, the redhead, is moving away.
She found a cheaper apartment elsewhere. She is packing
up her belongings. The rest of the street is dark, bereft.
In this world, nothing is ruled out & nothing is certain.
A savage carnivorous primate bloated with arrogance
floating about on a tiny island
among the trillions of islands out in the darkness.
Did you know that the human brain was larger 40 millennia back?
Does that mean they were smarter?
It stands to reason they were but we simply don't know.
& what of the marriage dance of the scorpion?
Do whales breach from exuberance
or for some sort of navigational reason?
What does the ant queen know or do to provoke such undying devotion?
What of the coelacanth & the neopilina—
not a fossil trace for 300 million years
then one day there she is swimming around.
In the mangrove swamps the fruit-bats hang from the trees
& flutter their great black wings.
How does a turnip sprout from a seed?
Creatures that hatch out of eggs & walk about on the earth
as if of their own volition.
How does a leaf unwind on its stem & turn red in the fall

& drop like a feather onto the snowy fields of the spinning world?
What does the shaman whisper into the ear of the beetle
that the beetle repeats to the rain?
Why does the common moth so love the light she is willing to die?
Is it some incurable hunger for warmth?
At least that I can understand.
How & why does the salmon swim thousands of miles back
to find the precise streambed, the very rock
under which it was born? God knows what that urge is
to be home in one's bed if only to die. There have been dogs,
abandoned by families moving to other parts of the country,
who have followed thru intricate cities,
over the wildest terrain—exhausted & bloody & limping—
a trail that in no way could be said to exist,
to scratch at a door they had never seen,
months, in cases, even years later.
Events such as these cannot be explained.
If indeed we are made of the same stuff as sea kelp & stars,
what that stuff is we haven't any idea.
The very atom eludes us.
Is it a myth & the cosmos an infinite series of Chinese boxes,
an onion of unending minusculation?
What would it look like apart from the grid of the language—
cut loose from its names?
Is there no solid ground upon which to plant our molecular flag?
What of the microorganic civilizations
living their complex domestic histories out in the roots of our hair?
Is there life in the stars?
Are there creatures like us weeping in furnished rooms
out past the solar winds in the incalculable dark
where everything's spinning away from everything else?
Are we just configurations of energy pulsing in space?
As if that explained this!
Is the universe conscious? Have we lived other lives?
Does the spirit exist? Is it immortal?
Do these questions even make sense?
& all this weighs on me like a verdict of exile.

I brush back the curtain an inch.
It flutters, as if by some ghostly hand.
Now Marie's light is off & the world is nothing again,
utterly vacant, *Sunyata*, the indecipherable void. How awesome
& sad & mysterious everything is tonight.
Tell me this, was the Shroud of Turin really the death-shroud of Jesus?
What of those tears that gush from the wounds of particular icons?
Don't tell me they don't. Thousands of people have seen them.
Did Therese Newman really survive on a wafer a day?
& the levitations of Eusapia Pallachino & St. Theresa?
& Salsky, who suffered the stigmata in that old Victorian house
on Oak Street across from the Panhandle on Good Friday.
With my own eyes I saw them—his palms full of blood.
Where does everything disappear that I loved?
The old friends with whom I would wander about
lost in rhapsodic babble, stoned, in the dark,
squabbling & giggling over the cosmos. That walk-up
on 7th Street overlooking the tenement roofs of Manhattan.
Lovely Elizabeth dead & Ronnie OD'd on a rooftop in Brooklyn
& Jerry killed in the war & the women—those dark,
furtive kisses & sighs, all the mysterious moanings of sex.
Where did I lose the addresses of all those people I knew?
Now even their names are gone: taken, lost, abandoned,
vanished into the blue. Where is the OED
I won at Brooklyn College for writing a poem
& the poem itself decades gone & the black & gold Madison
High School tennis team captain's jacket I was so proud of?
Where is that beaded headband? The marvelous Indian flute?
That book of luminous magic-marker paintings Eliot did?
& where is Eliot now? & Greg Marquez? & Marvin Torfield?
Where are the folding scissors from Avenida Abancay in Lima?
Where is the antique pocket watch Rosalind Eichenstein gave me—
I loved it so—the painted shepherd playing the flute
in the greenest, most diminutive hills.
I bet some junkie on 7th Street took it
but there's no way now to find out. It just disappeared
& no one & nothing that's lost will ever be back.

How came a cuneiform tablet unearthed by the Susquehanna?
Why was Knossos never rebuilt?
What blast flattened the Tunguska forest in 1908?
& those things that fall from the sky: manna
from heaven & toads & huge blocks of ice & alabaster
& odd-shaped gelatinous matter—fafrotskis of every description
& type that at one time or another have fallen out of the sky.
The alleged Venezuelan fafrotski—what is it exactly
& where did it come from?
& quarks & quasars & black holes. . . . The woolly mammoth,
one moment peacefully grazing on clover in sunlight,
an instant later quick-frozen into the arctic
antediluvian north. What inconceivable cataclysm occurred?
How did it happen?
What would my own children have looked like?
Why is there always one shoe on the freeway?
Why am I shivering? What am I even doing writing this poem?
Is it all nothing but ego—my name screaming out
from the grave? I look out the window again.
How strange, now the tobacco shop on the corner is lit.
A gaunt, mustachioed figure steps to the doorway & looks up
at my window & waves. It's Fernando Pessoa!
I wave back—Fernando! Fernando! I cry out.
But he doesn't see me. He can't. The light snaps off.
The tobacco shop disappears into the blackness, into the past. . . .
Who was the ghost in the red cape who told Henry IV he would die?
What of those children raised by wolves & gazelles?
What of spontaneous human combustion—those people
who burst into flame? Is space really curved?
Did the universe have a beginning
or did some sort of primal matter always exist?
Either way it doesn't make sense!
How does the pion come tumbling out of the void
& where does it vanish once it is gone?
& we too—into what & where do we vanish?
For the worms, surely we too are meat on the hoof.
Frankly it scares me, it scares the hell out of me.

The back of my neck is dripping with sweat . . . a man with a fever
located somewhere along the Pacific Coast
in the latter half of the 20th century by the Gregorian calendar:
a conscious, momentary configuration;
a bubble in the stew, a child of the dark.
I am going to stand up now if I can, that's what I'm going to do,
& make my way to the kitchen
& find the medicine Mary told me was there.
Perhaps she was right. Perhaps it will help me to sleep.
Yes, that's what I'll do—I'll sleep & forget.
We know only the first words of the message—if that.
I could weep when I think of how lovely it was
in its silver case all engraved with some sort of floral design,
the antique watch that Rosalind gave me years ago
on the Lower East Side of Manhattan
when we were young & in love & had nothing but time—
that watch with its little shepherd playing a flute
on a tiny hillside. Gone now like everything else.
Where in the name of Christ did it disappear to—
that's what I want to know!

## Credo

I am of those who believe
different things on different days.

## Hell

I died & went to Hell & it was nothing like L.A.
The air all shimmering & blue. No windows
busted, gutted walk-ups, muggings, rapes.
No drooling hoodlums hulking in the doorways.
Hell isn't anything like Ethiopia or Bangladesh or Bogota:
beggars are unheard of, no one's starving, nobody
lies moaning in the streets. Nor is it Dachau
with its ovens, Troy in flames, some slaughterhouse
where screaming animals, hung upside down, are bled & skinned.
No plague-infested Avignon or post-annihilation Hiroshima.
Quite the contrary: in Hell everybody's health is fine
forever, & the weather is superb—eternal spring.
The countryside all wild flowers & the cities
hum with commerce: cargo ships bring all the latest
in appliances, home entertainment, foreign culture, silks.
Folks fall in love, have children. There is sex
& romance for the asking. In a word, the place is perfect.
Only, unlike heaven, where when it rains
the people are content to let it rain,
in Hell they live like we do—endlessly complaining.
Nothing as it is is ever right. The astroturf
a nuisance, neighbors' kids too noisy, traffic
nothing but a headache. If the patio were just
a little larger, or the sunroof on the Winnebago worked.
If only we had darker eyes or softer skin or longer legs,
lived elsewhere, plied a different trade, were slender,
sexy, wealthy, younger, famous, loved, athletic—
Friend, I swear to you as one who has returned
if only to bear witness: No satanic furies
beat their kited wings. No bats shriek overhead.

There are no flames. No vats of boiling oil
wait to greet us in that doleful kingdom.
Nothing of the sort. The gentleman who'll ferry you across
is all solicitude & courtesy. The river black but calm.
The crossing less eventful than one might have guessed.
Though no doubt you will think it's far too windy on the water.
That the glare is awful. That you're tired, hungry, ill
at ease, or that—if nothing else—the quiet is unnerving:
that you need a drink, a cigarette, a cup of coffee.

## A Miracle

If waking with a simple toothache is enough
to make life miserable, imagine
how unpleasant it will be awakening from death;
how horrible to find yourself in such a cramped
& moldy little box,
dressed up in someone else's pants
& shoes, your toes & fingers freezing
as the name you had depended on
for your entire life is quietly erased.
No sound above that heavy lid but rain,
or gravel shifting into place.
What you wouldn't give to feel a little warmth,
to twist a bit & stretch, to taste
a drop of water, coffee, juice . . . anything
that might unparch the crumbling
blister that had been your mouth.
If only you had understood—how utterly miraculous
your ordinary life would have appeared!
You would have strolled about the city
marveling at every color, every face.
The smallest bug that crawled across your thumb
would send you into gasps of ecstasy,
so that you'd laugh & weep by turns
for no apparent reason, unashamed,
while those who knew you
wouldn't know what to make of it,
though in your company feel strangely blessed,
not in the least put out
by all your tenderness & sighs & desperate hugs.
"—Why, what an odd duck!" they'd laugh
& shake their heads.
"Whatever in the world's got into you?"

## Kowit

Sometimes when I'm not there to defend myself
the friends start playing *Kowit*.
Right from the start, the game,
begun with what seemed nothing
if not innocent affection,
takes a nasty turn:
from quietly amused to openly derisive,
ruthless, scathing, & at last
maniacally sadistic—
a psychopathic bacchanal of innuendo,
malice & vindictive lies.
It's jealousy & spite is what it is, of course.
They're rankled by my talent & integrity,
the editors & fancy women who surround me.
So Kowit's torn upon the rack
& barbecued alive
& chewed out of his skin like a salami
till there is nothing left of him
but blood & phlegm & scat
& fingernails & teeth,
& the famous Kowit penis
which is passed about the room
to little squeals of laughter
like a ridiculous hat.

## The Poetry Reading Was a Disaster

& I had expected so much.
All the big kahunas would be there—
the New York literati & foundation honchos
& publishing magi & hordes of insouciant groupies
& millions of poets—
the shaggy vanguard in green Adidas snapping their fingers,
surrealists whirling about by the ceiling
like adipose St. Theresas in mufti,
Bolinas cowboys & tatterdemalion beatniks
& Buddhists with mandarin beards & big goofy eyes
& Iowa poets in blazers & beanies
& Poundians nodding gigantic foreheads.
What tumultuous applause would erupt when I stepped
to the stage. What a thunder of adoration!
The room would be shaking.
The very city would tremble.
The whole damn Pacific plate start to shudder.
One good jolt & everything west of the San Andreas
would squirt back into Mesopotamian waters
& this time for good—
jesus but they would love me!
. . . Except when I got to the place it was tiny,
a hole in the wall,
& only a handful had shown up
& as soon as I walked to the front of the room
a kid started whining,
a chap in the second row fell asleep
& a trashed-out punk rocker with a swastika T-shirt,
drool on his chin & arms down to his knees
started cackling out loud. The razor blade
chained at his throat bounced up & down.
Somewhere a couple must have been screwing around
under their seats—I heard tongues
lapping it up, orgasmic weeping,

groans that grew louder and louder.
The kid wouldn't shut up.
The sleeper started to snore.
Potato chip eaters in every direction
were groping around in tinfoil bags
while the poetry lover, my host,
was oohing & aahing in all the wrong places.
I looked up politely. Couldn't they please,
please be a little more quiet?
Somebody snickered. There was a slap
& the brat started to bawl.
Someone stormed out in a huff slamming the door.
Another screamed that I was a pig & a sexist.
A heavy-set lady in thick Mensa glasses leaped to her feet
& announced that she was a student of Mark Strand.
In the back, the goon with the tattooed shirt
& the blade was guffawing & flapping his wings.
What could I do?
I read for all I was worth, straight from the heart,
all *duende* & dazzle—
no one & nothing was going to stop me!
Inspired at last, I read to a room
that had fallen utterly silent.
They must have been awed.
I wailed to the winds like Cassandra,
shoring our language against the gathering dark.
I raged at the heavens themselves
& ended the last set in tears, on my knees. . . .
When I looked up it was night & I was alone
except for an old lady up on a stepladder
scrubbing what looked like glops of dung off the wall
& humming.
The place stank of ammonia.
*Thank you so much*
had been scribbled over my briefcase in lipstick
or blood. Someone had stepped on my glasses,
lifted my wallet,

& sliced off all of my buttons,
half of my mustache,
& one of my balls.

## Lurid Confessions

One fine morning they move in for the pinch
& snap on the cuffs—just like that.
Turns out they've known all about you for years,
have a file the length of a paddy wagon
with everything—tapes, prints, film . . .
the whole shmear. Don't ask me how but
they've managed to plug a mike into one of your molars
& know every felonious move & transgression
back to the very beginning, with ektachromes
of your least indiscretion & peccadillo.
Needless to say, you are thrilled,
though sitting there in the docket
you bogart it, tough as an old tooth—
your jaw set, your sleeves rolled
& three days of stubble. . . . Only,
when they play it back it looks different:
a life common & loathsome as gum stuck to a chair.
Tedious hours of you picking your nose,
scratching, eating, clipping your toenails. . . .
Alone, you look stupid; in public, your rapier
wit is slimy & limp as an old band-aid.
They have thousands of pictures of people around you
stifling yawns. As for sex—a bit
of pathetic groping among the unlovely & luckless:
a dance with everyone making steamy love in the dark
& you alone in a corner eating a pretzel.
You leap to your feet protesting
that's not how it was, they have it all wrong.
But nobody hears you. The bailiff
is snoring, the judge is cleaning his teeth,
the jurors are all wearing glasses with eyes painted open.
The flies have folded their wings & stopped buzzing.
In the end, after huge doses of coffee,
the jury is polled. One after another

they manage to rise to their feet
like narcoleptics in August, sealing your fate:
Innocent . . . innocent . . . innocent. . . . Right down the line.
You are carried out screaming.

## The Prodigal Son's Brother

who'd been steadfast as small change all his life
forgave the one who bounced back like a bad check
the moment his father told him he ought to.
After all, that's what being good means.
In fact, it was he who hosted the party,
bought the crepes & champagne,
uncorked every bottle. With each drink
another toast to his brother: ex-swindler, hit-man
& rapist. By the end of the night
the entire village was blithering drunk
in an orgy of hugs & forgiveness,
while he himself,
whose one wish was to be loved as profusely,
slipped in & out of their houses,
stuffing into a satchel their brooches & rings
& bracelets & candelabra.
Then lit out at dawn with a light heart
for a port city he knew only by reputation:
ladies in lipstick hanging out of each window,
& every third door a saloon.

## Lot's Kinky Daughters

were into everything—dildoes,
daisychains, muff
& buggery parties, team sex,
buff clubs—you name it.
Like everyone else in that scatterbrained town
they were out for a good time
till Yahweh, disgusted,
burnt Sodom out of the hills like a tick,
thinking to teach them all a valuable lesson.
That whole voluptuous city in flames
& Lot's wife,
bouncing about in the back of the pickup,
wedged in between the jacuzzi & sofa,
suddenly remembers Poopsie the cat
& looks back &—
well, you know the rest.
That night in a cave in the hills above Zoar,
Lot is sprawled out on that couch in a tizzy,
his simpleton daughters
down at his feet in their pj's
trying to figure it out.
"Well, it's mean if you ask me,"
the older one pouts. "Mama was nice
& this place is creepy & boring."
"It must have been some kind of lesson,"
the younger one adds. "But about what?"
& she yawns from the effort,
then reaching under the pillow
pulls out the blackberry schnapps
that she managed to salvage.
Two shots & they're lit
like a bordello switchboard on payday,
the three of them cackling & panting
& ripe to kindle the tribes

of Ben Ami & Moab—
their shadows in candlelight
folding together & swirling about
like some sort of angel—
but darker, with translucent limbs,
& misshapen wings,
& immense genitalia.

# Pranks

A Catholic magazine says the reported apparitions of the Virgin Mary in Yugoslavia are a "joke that got out of hand." The publication, *Fidelity*, contends the apparitions began as a prank.

*San Diego Tribune*

As it turned out, life in Paradise wasn't so awful:
Joseph was with her, the neighbors were absolute angels,
& Jesus, despite his morbid obsession with sin,
was still a good-natured kid.
About the only one up there she couldn't stand at all
was old Bloodbath himself. Whenever she heard he was planning
some really icky disaster she made sure not to watch.
Instead, she would keep herself busy interceding for widows,
blessing the poor, & minding her candles.
Nonetheless, there were times when the afterlife
seemed as thin as a wafer—& as tasteless & flat.
On such occasions, like anyone else,
she'd long for a little vacation, some old-fashioned fun.
Which is why now & then she would swoop back to Earth,
where life, for all of its anguish, was seething with passion.
She'd appear in a grotto, or up on a cloud,
or surrounded by roses inside a young Indian's cape.
Or she'd squirt little drops on the cheeks of one of her statues.
Her favorite joke though was jumping out of the bushes at kids
& telling them all to be good.
Then she'd vanish &, giggling, watch from a distance
as pilgrims would come by the boatload
to kiss everything that they could where the miracle happened.
The old folks & cripples were dear, though the ones
who crawled on their bellies she liked even better.
Unfortunately, though it seemed at the time like a harmless
diversion, it simply increased eight-hundred fold
the number of desperate prayers she had to say *No* to.
Which made her so sad she wished she had never dreamt up
that gag in the first place. There must, she thought

to herself, be less unpleasant pranks she could pull.
Which is why, some mornings on Earth,
you'll see all of the trash cans upended,
or walking along to the bus stop you'll suddenly get wonked
on the head with a water balloon or a snowball.
& nights when the doorbell rings & you get out of bed
only to find that there's nobody there,
don't just stand in the doorway
muttering under your breath about rotten neighborhood kids,
but take in the bracing night air & the shimmering darkness
until, despite the dreadful joke of this world, you remember
how precious & rare & marvelous everything is,
& vow from then on to be just as happy & good as you possibly can—
though where that thought came from you won't have any idea.
What a silly mood I am in, you'll think to yourself,
as millions of stars wink over your head
& the crooked grin of a crescent moon pops over the roofs.

## How the Other Thief Got into Heaven


When Jesus got back to heaven, the thief to whom he had promised
Paradise up on the cross was already there. But the candelabra
that had stood on either side of the mantel downstairs in the throne room
were missing. So were Jehovah's gold pocket watch & his silver cigar box,
the one that when you lifted the lid played Handel's *Messiah*.
Oddly enough, the thief attempted neither to run nor to hide,
but was unconcernedly down on his knees in the chapel piously praying.
Accused, he owned up at once. Well, of course! he explained.
For someone like me what else could Paradise mean
but heavy gold & windows with cheap locks?
But . . . but those things have been in the family for aeons—why, almost forever!
Jesus exclaimed, momentarily flustered & shaking his head.
Why you can't—I mean—the very idea—
Okay, okay already, the other one answered. Look,
if you want I should give up my calling, consider it done.
But if you're asking me to get the swag back, you can forget it.
It's out of the question. I mean there are middlemen, fences . . . Believe me,
the guys who work for the syndicate don't make returns.
But they have to! cried Jesus. You don't know what the old man is like
when he's riled! Remember Gomorrah? The Flood? The Amalekite Kingdom?
Hmmm, mused the thief. I suppose if my buddy were up here to help me . . .
Your buddy?
Yeah. You remember, the guy they hammered up on the cross to your left.
Believe me, this is just the sort of caper he could pull off.
So, I'm thinking if he could be sent for . . .
Impossible! Jesus protested. That fellow neither believed nor repented!
Well, if that's how you feel, shrugged the thief, suit yourself.
I mean none of that stuff was in cherry condition to start with . . .
But this is outrageous! cried Jesus. It's bald-faced extortion!
Loving thy neighbor's how I see it, snapped back the thief.
Me & my buddy we go back a long ways . . .
Oh for heaven's sake! Jesus threw up his hands
at which very instant the reprobate under discussion suddenly
popped out of nowhere to find himself standing beside them, unshaven

& flushed & stinking more than a little of sulfur but flashing
a big toothless grin nonetheless.
Now, whether Jesus was all that upset or simply putting it on
for appearance's sake is still much disputed by biblical scholars.
What isn't at issue, however, is that the two rogues, reunited in heaven,
started dancing around in a frenzy of whoops & backslaps,
high-fives & hollers, as gleeful as if they had finally hit the perfecta.
As for the stuff he had heisted, the thief slapped his forehead.
Heaven forfend! How foolish of me to've forgotten! Why I do believe the loot
is just where I left it, right over here in the baptismal font
wrapped up in Jehovah's long-johns.
& fishing them out he handed back every last item: wetter for sure,
but apparently no worse for wear—the antique watch still, in fact,
merrily ticking—so that Jehovah, upon his return the next evening,
had no idea whatsoever they'd ever been gone.
Though even without that you can be certain the old man
found no lack of reason to work himself into a lather
in which he proceeded to pummel this world with eruptions & famine &
mayhem & plague & every which sort of calamitous woe—in his usual manner.

## Madly Singing in the Mountains

Fred Moramarco & I had been hiking
up in the Cuyamacas,
lost in our usual babble, boring
more holes in the world than the woodpeckers do:
talking the angels out of their halos,
the muses out of their tutus,
the world into marshmallow pudding.
From post-deconstructionist theory
& newfangledness in poetics,
we'd moved on to Salvadoran death squads
& low-intensity warfare;
the legions of evangelical zealots out on the streets
agitating for more executions,
compulsory prayer, ironclad regulations
against miscegenation & condoms—
a jihad against homosexual teachers,
the ACLU, & *The Bob Dylan Songbook*.
They wanted fellatio outlawed,
the braceros deported,
the fossil records revoked.
The trail we'd been hiking had swung northwest
thru stands of black oak,
till suddenly it opened onto a ridge
& we stepped thru a tunnel of branches
into broad daylight.
The sky impossibly blue.
East—mountains that rolled on forever;
west—where the light was hazier still,
the mesa dissolving into a mist
we supposed was the coast. Fred
thought he could almost make out the ocean,
though at that distance, in that light,
whatever was out there had faded
into the gray Pacific wash of the void:

one of those moments when,
stunned by the infinite, everything stops.
"Jesus," Fred sighed, "I'm glad
we got out here today."
& I nodded "Yeah, me too, me too!"
& before we even knew we had been there,
were back into Jimmy Swaggart
& Schrödinger's Cat;
the friendship of Po Chu-I & Yuan Chen;
those child prodigies: Mozart, Arthur Rimbaud
& Tracie Lords; no-fault divorce;
every-moment awareness; Muji—the first gate;
the marriage of Chaos & Form;
& the hypothetical origins of carbon-based life.
In such manner making our way
to where Green Valley Falls
tumbles into the Sweetwater River Canyon.
We too merrily babbling away—tongues
like party-streamers in high wind.
Delighted. Oblivious. Full steam ahead.

## The Workout

Decked out in purple shorts & spandex tights
& party-colored jogging suits,
the votaries of fitness have been trying to shape up.
While dervishes of Monday evening high-impact
aerobics jerk & twitch like frenzied zealots
in convulsive seizure, & those dumbbell lifters,
grunting into full-length mirrors at their own
sweet pumped-up repetitions,
spend their workouts flirting with themselves,
other flagellants have strapped their limbs
to squat-&-flex devices, chest expanders, hip
& thigh racks, & are climbing dutifully
the gravitronic exer-stairway up toward skinny heaven.
Not unlike the penitents of other sects,
they are convinced that decades of decay
can be undone, & that the more one genuflects
the less one rots—a doctrine
that has got the aged, the adipose & the misshapen
pedaling their stationary bikes
in such unholy fury you would think
they were outracing Time—that hag
who has been waiting at the finish line to snip the thread
& will not be outrun—
while every now & then some sleek
young thing in leotards parades her killer body
to remind the women what they do not look like,
& the men, what they are not about to have
the pleasures of, however long they bicycle in place.
A carnival of dreams is all it is—
this imbecilic adoration of the golden calf

& bulging chest & tapered thigh,
this robegalia of compulsive nitwits & deluded fools—
is just what I am thinking when I spot him
riding toward me in that mirror, flushed & puffing:
my unpleasant-looking older cousin
with that stupid grin,
as smug & supercilious as ever: haggard,
baggy-eyed & self-impressed, his drooping
middle thicker than I'd ever have supposed.
Humiliated, frankly, to be seen with him,
especially in such a place as this,
I turn my gaze discreetly elsewhere, for god knows
we never have had all that much in common—
I being by a long shot younger,
more athletic, slender, muscular & better-looking.

## Madness & Civilization

Half-mad with impatience (she was
already a good
hour late), & thinking perhaps
that she hadn't been able
to find the right hallway
or wing (that is to say, grasping
at straws), I bolted
out of my chair
& flung open the door
of my office—to nothing:
the exit sign
flickering over the stairwell,
& echoing thru that long, desolate hall,
the voice of some pedant
three classrooms down,
beating his students to death
with Foucault & de Man:

                how the shifting structures
of language & culture
had rendered the old texts
indecipherable:
           *"Which means,*
      *don't you see,*
      *that even our own early modernist writers*
      *are all but incomprehensible now!"*

           Would she never show up?
I slammed the door on that clown
& made my way back to my desk.
So much for expectation, desire, confused
middle age—so much
for our long-
awaited appointment to touch

up her paper
on Dante's Francesca.

I dropped to my chair,
resigned, I suppose,
to wait there forever,
an old fool
choking on lust & despair,
as manic & wracked as Catullus
hunting that minx thru every alley in Rome.

    Izumi Shikibu says
in a poem a thousand years old,
that having spent her whole night
waiting for him
she would have flung open her door
had so much as a water-rail knocked.

& I know what she means.
& it sticks in my heart like a spike.

    Like Pound, *il miglior fabbro,*
I had over-prepared the event.

## Some Clouds

Now that I've unplugged the phone
no one can reach me—
At least for this one afternoon
they will have to get by without my advice or opinion.
Now nobody else is going to call
& ask in a tentative voice
if I haven't yet heard that she's dead,
that woman I once loved—
nothing but ashes scattered over a city
that barely itself any longer exists.
Yes, thank you, I've heard.
It had been too lovely a morning.
That in itself should have warned me.
The sun lit up the tangerines
& the blazing poinsettias
like so many candles.
For one afternoon they will have to forgive me.
I am busy watching things happen again
that happened a long time ago,
as I lean back in Josephine's lawn chair
under a sky of incredible blue,
broken—if that is the word for it—
by a few billowing clouds,
all white & unspeakably lovely,
drifting out of one nothingness into another.

## Jacumba

I am sitting in the restaurant of the spiffy
new air-conditioned Jacumba Motel
& Health Spa, sipping a root beer
& staring out at a desert
so blazingly desiccated & stark
it's hard to imagine that anything
other than lizards & buckthorn survives here,
& wondering where the old Jacumba Hotel
disappeared to,
that rambling, stucco monstrosity
where one summer night we—
well, what's the use. Without that hotel
this town is nothing at all of the crumbling,
moth-infested ghost town it was,
blistering out in the Anza-Borrego,
halfway to Yuma,
exquisitely shabby & brooding.
Ah, Time—with your ferocious improvements!
Your infernal, confounded meddling!

## A Whitman Portrait


You know that portrait of him that caused such a ruckus?
The one where he's propped in a cane-back chair
striking a pose so grave & heroic
you'd swear at first glance it was Odin or Lear or—
ah, but at that very moment you'll notice,
as just about everyone finally does,
the butterfly perched on his right index finger.
& then you can see that Walt's sitting there
under that rakish sombrero & beard, grandly amused,
as much as to say: *How splendid it is to see you, my dear,*
*& what a propitious moment to call. . . .*
You can guess how his critics stewed over that one!
They'd fling up their arms in maniacal fury
& swear up & down that the thing was a fraud.
Why, it's nothing but papier-mâché, they would shriek.
A cardboard & wire photographer's prop!
Which slander, however absurd & transparent,
the populace simply assumed to be fact—
till just last September when high-resolution spectro-
analysis proved what any fool could have guessed:
she was just what she seemed, mortal & breathing,
a carbon-molecular creature like us: *Papilio*
*aristodamus*, now all but extinct;
the very swallowtail, golden-banded & blue-tipped,
that archeo-lepidopterists claim
could have been seen all over Camden that summer:
one of the millions scooting about thru the woods
& fields around Timber Creek Pond. Only, for whatever
odd reason, this one had taken a fancy to Walt.
When she wasn't flitting about in the fennel & parsley,
the neighbors would see her light on his wrist
or swing thru his beard, or perch on his shoulder
like some sort of angel, or sprite, or familiar.
How he did it we don't know exactly,

but as the photographer set up his camera
Walt sat himself down by the open window
& hummed a few bars of Donizetti's *La Favorita*,
at which simple tune that bright little beauty
flitted in from the garden as if she'd been called to.
If it's true there exist fake butterflies
cut out of paper & wire, my guess is
they belong to a later generation of poets.
In any case, this one was made of the same stuff
as we are—felt pleasure & pain in abundance:
lit first on the broad brim of his hat, next
at his knee, & at last on his finger. Was greeted by Walt
with a gruff, friendly laugh as one of his cronies—
at which precise instant the chap with the camera
(he could hardly believe his remarkable luck)
pulled down the lever that triggered the shutter—
preserving forever that singular flight
of felicitous whimsy—this portrait at once majestic
& tender & bathed in affection & grace & delight:
Walt Whitman & butterfly. Camden, New Jersey. 1883.

## Solo Monk

One day back in the 60s, Monk was sitting at the piano,
Charlie Mingus pulling at his coat
how Monk should put the word in so the Mingus group
could play the Five Spot, seeing as how
Monk's already legendary gig down there was ending—Mingus,
all persuasion & cajolery, ran it down for twenty minutes
till he capped it with the comment:
    "Dig it, Thelonious,
                  you know we Black Brothers
            GOT to stick together!"
At which point Monk, laconic to a fault
(till then he hadn't said a word), turned
slowly with a sidewise glance & raised one eyebrow.
                  "Ma-aan,"
          he said
"I thought you was Chi-nese!"

& evenings, between sets,
Monk would pace outside the Five Spot,
head cocked to some inner keyboard.
With that listing gait of his, that wispy black goatee,
that rumpled herringbone tweed hat
he sported in those days,
he'd pace that corner, solitary
& quixotic
        in a rapture
                of exploding chords—
                    all angular
      & dissonant
        & oddly phrased.

One summer night a Checker Cab
pulled up as he was so engaged
& Monk, who happened to be passing at that moment,

swung back the door,
then stepped so quietly & self-effacingly behind it
that you would have thought it was his calling—
but his ear as ever cocked to that imaginary keyboard.
                An elegant patrician couple, clubbing,
—blond Westchester money—
stepped out on 8th Street like an ad for Chivas Regal.
As the primped fox sashayed past him in her saffron
strapless, tossing back her golden mane,
her escort nodded vaguely, not so much as glancing up
at that solicitous, albeit altogether funky-
looking colored doorman
                        with the goofy hat.
A gesture almost too indifferent to be haughty.
& with that they hurried past & disappeared
into the Five Spot,
having come to hear the legendary Monk, that droll
& idiosyncratic piano.
                *The sensation*, Whitney Balliett wrote,
        *of missing*
*the bottom step in the dark.*
                        "—Eerie, isn't it,
                        to hear him playing
                        though he's dead,"
Mary said, playing Monk
the night we heard he had died.
& she lowered the dust cover over the turntable
as quietly as Monk had shut the door
of that Checker Cab
& turning without sign or gesture
had gone off bopping down the street,
head cocked as ever to one side
& circled by the halo of that rumpled hat:
                oblivious . . .
                        preoccupied . . .
                                lost

in the sweet jazz of the night—
                              Monk
              on 8th Street
        at the end of summer
in the early 60s.
                         Must have been around 11:55.

## I Attend a Poetry Reading

The fellow reading poetry at us wouldn't stop.
Nothing would dissuade him:
not the stifling heat; the smoky walls
with their illuminated clocks;
our host, who shifted anxiously
from foot to foot.
Polite applause had stiffened
to an icy silence:
no one clapped
or nodded.
No one sighed.
Surely he must understand that we had families
waiting for us, jobs
we had to get to in the morning.
That chair was murdering my back.
The cappuccino
tasted unaccountably of uric acid.
Lurid bullfight posters flickered
in the red fluorescent light—
& suddenly I knew that I had died,
& for those much too windy readings of my own
had been condemned
to sit forever in this damned cafe.
A squadron of enormous flies
buzzed around the cup of piss
I had been drinking from.
Up at the mike, our poet of the evening
grinned,
& flicked his tail,
& kept on reading.

## Still Life

For an hour he's been pacing back & forth
between the double-latched front door
& living room,
insisting that he has to leave,
that Gertie's waiting downstairs with the car.
Patiently, my mother tries to coax
him back into his chair—then suddenly
explodes: Mickey, please,
you're driving me insane.
Take your jacket off & just sit down!
Your sister has been dead for thirty years. . . .
& then starts sobbing
uncontrollably.
Contrite, all that belligerence
knocked out of him, my dutiful
& gentle father—old,
confused—sits beside her on the couch
& takes her hand.
All right, he says, I won't go anywhere. . . .
So there they sit—together, holding hands.
It's night. Beyond the spathiphyllum
at the window—white
sail with its single flower—
downtown Philly's skyline
etched in light,
somewhere near the end of the millennium.

## Last Will

If I am ever
unlucky enough to die
(God forbid!),
I would like to be propped up
in my orange overstuffed chair
with my legs crossed,
dressed in a cashmere sweater
& jeans,
& embalmed
in a permanent glaze
like a donut,
or Lenin,
a small bronze plaque
on the door of my study
showing the dates
of my incarnation & death.
& leave the room as it was!
Let nothing be touched in the house!
My underpants stuck on the doorknob
just where I left them.
My dental floss
lying on top of the Bhagavad Gita
next to my socks.
Let the whole of Ebers Street
be roped off
& planted with yews
from Narragansett to Cape May
& left as a monument to my passing.
The street?
No—the city itself!
Henceforth
let it be known
as the Steve M. Kowit
Memorial Park & Museum.

Better yet
if the thing can be done
without too much fuss
put the whole planet to sleep.
Let the pigeons and busses
& lawyers & ladies
hanging out wash
freeze in their tracks.
Let the whole thing
be preserved under ice
just as it looked
when the last bit of drool
trickled under my chin.
Let the last of the galaxies
sizzle out
like a match in the wind
& the cosmic balloon
shrink down to a noodle
& screech to a halt.
Let time itself clot
like a pinprick of blood
& the great solar flame
flicker down
to the size of a *yahrzeit* candle
leaving the universe dark
but for one tiny spotlight
trained on the figure of me
propped in my chair—
for after my death
what possible reason could life
in any form
care to exist?
Don't you see,
it would be utterly pointless!
I would be gone!
Look, try to conceive it,
a world without me! Me

entirely absent—
nobody here with these eyes,
this name,
these teeth!
Nothing but vacant space,
a dry sucking wind
where I walked,
where I sat—Where
you used to see me
you would see nothing at all—
I tell you it dwarfs the imagination . . .
Oh yes, one last thing:
the right leg
is to be crossed over the left
—I prefer it that way—
& poised on the knee.
Prop the left elbow up
on the arm of the chair
with a pen
in my right hand—
let my left
be characteristically
scratching my skull
or pulling my hair.
If you wish,
close the lids of my eyes
but whatever you do
the mouth must remain open
just as it was in life—
Yes,
open forever!
On that I absolutely insist!

## Notice

This evening, the sturdy Levis
I wore every day for over a year
& which seemed to the end
in perfect condition,
suddenly tore.
How or why I don't know,
but there it was: a big rip at the crotch.
A month ago my friend Nick
walked off a racquetball court,
showered,
got into his street clothes,
& halfway home collapsed & died.
Take heed, you who read this,
& drop to your knees now & again
like the poet Christopher Smart
& kiss the earth & be joyful
& make much of your time
& be kindly to everyone,
even to those who do not deserve it.
For although you may not believe
it will happen,
you too will one day be gone.
I, whose Levis ripped at the crotch
for no reason,
assure you that such is the case.
Pass it on.

## The Blue Dress

When I grab big Eddie, the gopher drops from his teeth
& bolts for the closet, vanishing
into a clutter of shoes & valises & vacuum
attachments, & endless boxes of miscellaneous rubbish.
Grumbling & cursing, carton by carton,
I lug everything out:
that mountain of hopeless detritus—until,
with no place to hide, he breaks
for the other side of the room & I have him at last,
trapped in a corner, tiny & trembling.
I lower the plastic freezer bowl over his head &

                                              *Boom!*—

slam the thing down.
                                "Got him!" I yell out,
slipping a folder under the edge for a lid.
But when I open the front door, it's teeming,
a rain so fierce it drives me back into the house,
& before I can wriggle into my sneakers,
Mary, impatient, has grabbed the contraption
out of my hands & run off into the yard with it, barefoot.
She's wearing that blue house dress.
I know just where she's headed: that big
mossy boulder down by the oleanders
across from the shed,
& I know what she'll do when she gets there—hunker
down, slip off the folder,
let the thing slide to the ground
while she speaks to him softly, whispers
encouraging, comforting things.
Only after the gopher takes a few tentative steps,
dazed, not comprehending how he got back
to his own world, then tries to run off,
will she know how he's fared: if he's wounded,
or stunned, or okay—depraved ravisher
of our gladiolus & roses, but neighbor & kin nonetheless.

Big Eddie meows at my feet while I stand
by the window over the sink, watching
her run back thru the rain,
full of good news. Triumphant. Laughing. Wind
lashing the trees. It's hard to fathom
how gorgeous she looks, running like that
through the storm: that blue
sheath of a dress aglow in the smoky haze—
that luminous blue dress pasted by rain to her hips.
I stand at the window grinning, amazed
at my own undeserved luck—
at a life that I still, when I think of it, hardly believe.

VOLUME 1: *One Hand on the Wheel* by Dan Bellm
VOLUME 2: *In Danger* by Suzanne Lummis
VOLUME 3: *The Dumbbell Nebula* by Steve Kowit
VOLUME 4: *Listening to Winter* by Molly Fisk

The *California Poetry Series* was created to showcase and document the literary energy of the Golden State, and to celebrate the wide range of aesthetics, cultures, and geography in California poetry. The books feature work by poets with strong ties to California. Four volumes will be released annually. The series is a collaboration: Malcolm Margolin, Heyday Books, is publisher. Joyce Jenkins, *Poetry Flash,* is series editor.

An advisory board of prominent poets and cultural leaders has been assembled to encourage and support California poetry through this book series. These include Alfred Arteaga, Chana Bloch, Christopher Buckley, Marilyn Chin, Karen Clark, Wanda Coleman, Gillian Conoley, Peter Coyote, Jim Dodge, Lawrence Ferlinghetti, Jack Foley, Jewelle Gomez, Robert Hass, Jane Hirshfield, Fanny Howe, Lawson Inada, Jaime Jacinto, Diem Jones, Stephen Kessler, William Kistler, Carolyn Kizer, Steve Kowit, Dorianne Laux, Philip Levine, Genny Lim, Suzanne Lummis, Lewis MacAdams, David Mas Masumoto, David Meltzer, Deena Metzger, Carol Muske-Dukes, Jim Paul, Kay Ryan, Richard Silberg, Gary Snyder, Dr. Kevin Starr, David St. John, Sedge Thomson, Alan Williamson, and Gary Young.

*California Poetry Series* books are available at bookstores nationwide or by subscription ($40.00/year). For more information:
Heyday Books
P.O. Box 9145
Berkeley, California 94709
phone: 510.549.3564    fax: 510.549.1889
e-mail: roundhouse@heydaybooks.com

CALIFORNIA POETRY SERIES

3